I0711442

HOW WE ENDED THE SQUIRREL WAR PEACEABLY

By Robert F. Burgess

Spyglass Publications
308 W. Marion Street
Chattahoochee, Florida 32324

HOW WE ENDED
THE SQUIRREL WAR
PEACEABLY

By ROBERT F. BURGESS

**SPYGLASS PUBLICATIONS,
CHATTAHOOCHEE, FLORIDA**

A 2020 Paperback edition

Published by:

Robert F. Burgess
Spyglass Publications
308 West Marion Street
Chattahoochee, Florida 32324

Cover photograph and history courtesy Wikipedia
Cover Design © Robert F. Burgess
Author photo by Charles Harnage Jr.

Dedicated to the Memory of my Always Faithful Friends
Cicero, Lindy, Pal, Smut, Strega, Chita, Tisha, Smokey and
Pooky who always made us happy.

CONTENTS

1 Welcome to My Squirrel War

At 10 A.M. on a cool mid-July morning in Northwest Florida my electronic squirrel detector shrieked its two-toned warning: **"Beep-Boop! Beep-Boop! Beep-Boop!"** and a red light flashed. It kept squawking and flashing it saw so much mischief! Instantly I knew It was a raid by Our Gang of Four, the Sneaky Petes! I knew because I had seen it all before.

Four sleek racing gray squirrels that always attack together, silently dart from the thickets, moving fast like a tsunami, racing across the lawn to my carport, a family of four feisty scrappers: Pete 1, Pete 2, Pete 3 and Spanky, the youngest. It is their latest desperate hit-and-run attack with the two oldest brothers leading the way. These two make the lightening swift cat burglar pole-climbing and tight-rope walking moves on my feeder suspended high overhead while the two youngest stay on the ground awaiting the fallout.

With the alarm ringing in my ears I leap to my feet and race through the house to the back door. It's glass panels are cranked open and I stare at the bird feeder dangling in space overhead just inside the carport. The two cat burglars are already at the prize.

Skilled at what they do, the two oldest brothers triggered the alarm by climbing the 4-inch diameter 12-foot pipe carport roof support containing the prize. At its top they wrestled their way over a large pie pan barrier and balancing themselves precariously they crawled across that skinny taut clothesline tightrope for five feet. It led them to the suspended bird feeder dangling in space just inside the eaves of the carport.

One brother laid on the bird perch wrapped around the feeder and was busily raking sunflower seeds and millet out with a paw. It showered all over the ground for the waiting siblings. His next older brother was atop the feeder upside down climbing down to help him.

I jerk open the backdoor with a bang and screech, *"No, No, No, No! Get out, out, out! YOU'RE NOT BIRDS!"*

The thief atop the feeder shoots off into space. The one wrapped around the bird perch goes the wrong way into space right into my five-foot-long wind chimes that instantly sound off: **"BING, BANG, BONG, CLATTER, CLATTER!"**

The loudly mixed musical notes come when he discovers the pipes aren't something solid but in the confusion he still tries to climb them. When he realizes he can't, he too rockets off into space in the direction of his brother and all four brigands streak back across my lawn into the thickets they came from.

From behind a forest of miniature trees, with his trusty .45-caliber squirt gun, friend Jim Folds takes a bead on the fast disappearing sneaky squirrels that just attacked our Command Post.

Battlefield overview from the Command Post.

The enemy all escaped, getting home free, but not before hearing a few of my choice purple epitaphs hurled loudly at them as they left. Even the neighborhood dogs heard them and started barking excitedly. They wanted a piece of that action, whatever it was.

It made no difference. Every gray squirrel in the neighborhood was conditioned to react the same way. It was a well-rehearsed hit-and-run-operation. If I hadn't been home they'd have cleaned out the feeder to the last tinniest seed. When squirrels are involved a lot of birdseed disappears. Mine was going at the rate of 40 pounds every couple months. 240 pounds of feed a year. The squirrels got the bulk of it.

Nothing new about that. Thousands of birdfeeder enthusiasts across the country have the same problem. You enjoy watching the birds but not those pesky squirrels that keep the birds away from their food and wolf down the seeds themselves. That's why in one form or another we birders are all caught up in this mutual war against pillaging squirrels in our neighborhoods.

That's the point where I got serious about trying to do something about it. I began to plan how to block them effectively.

Things were about as ugly as they could get. Every time the enemy made these stealth attacks, they always began in deep silence. I've been reading in the carport 20 feet away from them and they would silently by-pass my squirrel-guards and be wrapped around their target without making a sound. Foggy days were especially bad. They worked close and stealthy then.

Foggy days bring the enemy closer ...just like Nam.

After a few of those times, I had to come up with some kind of warning system so I could catch them in the act and bombard them with some choice anti-squirrel words. They might not understand them but I guarantee you they understood my shouts and body language.

But what could I really do? Modern times called for modern methods. Something high tech that they might not figure out in just a matter of minutes the way they usually did. To begin with I needed something that would warn me the enemy was about their naughty business when I was in the house. I needed a secret warning alarm. So, I went high tech on them with a motion-detector. The sensor that reported any movement was aimed up that pipe supporting the roof of the carport. The alarm was in the house. Right from the start when they climbed that pipe my electronic surveillance unit instantly notified me of their presence.

If this squirrel tries to climb the pole toward the feeder that white motion sensor will trigger the alarm in the house.

This reminded me of the BAR trip-flare warnings we set up at night in northern Italy around a fully illuminated ammo dump during World War II.

After the shooting war Tito's Yugoslavian Partisans wanted that bunch of captured explosives we guarded on a mountaintop in Trieste. They often tried to steal it at night. The Partisans would cut the barbed wire and try to get at that big pile of explosives stacked in open-ended Quonset huts. So we surrounded the dump with trip flares. Whenever a flare fired Browning Automatic-Rifle squads raked the area with hot lead. Usually it was only a wild animal that had triggered the alarm. My setup was a bit more sophisticated. It was an early warning system that the enemy could not hear. It worked perfectly, much probably to the disappointment of my bushy-tailed raiders.

I bought it because for two nights something was

unscrewing the lid of a large plastic barrel of birdseed and leaving it on the ground beside it. None of the birdseed seemed disturbed. I might have forgotten it once but not twice. Harbor Freight sold these motion detectors so I rigged up one focused on the barrel at night. If the squirrels were smart enough to unscrew the lid to my 'ammo dump' I wanted to see it.

The first night the alarm beside my bed went off around 1:30 A.M. I grabbed a flashlight and hustled toward the kitchen backdoor.

There was nothing to see. I stood in the dark hardly breathing watching but saw nothing.

The alarm went off the second night about 2 A.M. I tiptoed through the house and in the darkness looked through the open glass louvers of my back door. Nothing, What was this? A ghost? Either that or a very sensitive night stalker. I held my breath. After a few moments a small dog-sized black shape moved past the barrel and was gone. He either heard or smelled me and was smart enough to leave. I suspected it was one or more raccoons since they are capable of such things. But birdseed for breakfast!

Next day I drilled a hole through the edge of the lid and the barrel, inserted a long spike and that was the end of any more mischief from my Midnight Marauder.

Despite this hullabaloo, I actually deep down don't dislike squirrels. We had been at war for some years now but growing up in Grand Rapids, Michigan as a kid I had a lot of squirrel friends. They were Fox squirrels up there and they helped clean up all the acorns that fell from trees in our yard. I doubt that they had any interest in birdseed at all. But they sure liked their nuts. I got to be such good friends with our squirrels that I could feed them by hand. All I had to do was tap a nut a few times on our sidewalk and the squirrels would come and take them from my hands. They always pulled back a couple feet, cracked and ate the nut while I watched. Then they would beg for more. I fed them a lot of nuts and all of us became fast friends.

But these Southern squirrels were a lot different. They were afraid of me, mainly because I always barked at them when they raided my feeders. Our carport where the current birdfeeder hung was a pleasant place to enjoy the cool breezes and to read. I put a table and four chairs out there and surrounded them with about a dozen of my Juniper bonsais. At one time I had 75 of these miniature trees scattered around my outdoor office building on an automatic watering system.

The first full-sized birdfeeder I made turned out to be squirrel-proof. Hung under the eaves of my small outdoor office building, the feeder was opposite my desktop window where I had a good view of bird activity. The feature that spelled defeat for marauding squirrels was a sheet of galvanized metal feeder roof that dumped them the moment they climbed down and set foot on it. Also since it hung under the eaves of my building it was 8 feet above ground and well out of a squirrel's jumping range.

2 War Stories

"Public Enemy Number One in America is a backyard one pound busybody with industrial-strength teeth and a luxuriously bushy tail: the gray squirrel." That's what author George H. Harrison said of them in his book titled, *SQUIRREL WARS: Backyard Wildlife Battles & How to Win Them.* His book includes one short chapter on the difficulties bird-lovers have with squirrels raiding their birdfeeders. This is one of fifteen chapters describing how others have solved their problems dealing with a variety of predators that may invade your garden.

War? Uh-uh, not me. I just like to eat birdseed.

Public Enemy Number One. Really?

Harrison goes on to say that "being challenged by a gray, four-footed, furry beast, people have nearly gone berserk in their attempt to outwit, out-maneuver, out-think, and out-perform gray squirrels. Some people have dedicated all of their free-time to 'keeping those blasted squirrels off my feeders.' Yet, gray squirrels continue to wreak havoc in backyards from coast to coast while the search for the perfect squirrel-proof bird feeder forges on."

The author advises never putting a birdfeeder anywhere near a tree that is taller than whatever supports the feeder because sooner or later a squirrel will jump from the tree to the feeder. He said that in Virginia a bird-lover who had just put up a new birdfeeder far enough from a distant tree said that he counted the times a hungry squirrel tried jumping from the tree to the feeder. He said that he jumped 47 times without making it. But on the 48th try the squirrel landed squarely on the feeder and from that time on he never missed again.

One bird lover I know was so incensed over the fact that his squirrels were cleaning out his feeder he got out his .22 rifle, loaded it with what is known as Rat Shot and took aim at a squirrel smirking at him on his feeder.

Just as the man pulled the trigger, the squirrel jumped off and the only thing that got blown away was the man's feeder.

In Bainbridge, Georgia a lady named Miss Pat, put out a dishful of the finest kind of squirrel food – a variety of unshelled nuts. Her squirrels must have thought she was Mrs. Claus for all the goodies she bequeathed upon them.

Her gift only lasted a couple days and then the dish was empty. When she looked out her window at them the squirrels stood beside the empty bowl and stared back at her until she refilled it. If she forgot, the squirrels all ended up on her windowsill where they left dirty paw prints on the glass until Miss Pat shaped up and got more of their chow into their bowl. This too kind lady had a tough time weaning the squirrels off their nutty habit. I believe she had to take a long vacation hoping that when she and the family returned the squirrels would NOT be inhabiting their house. They were fortunate. But she did have to switch to a birdfeeder and birdseed that the squirrels regularly raided.

One bird-lover came up with the idea of using a deer zapper and an electrical wire to keep the squirrels away from her father's favorite feeding place. That was a long outdoor railing where her father scattered seeds and the birds would come and get them while he watched through a curtained window.

The zapper sounded like a good idea. It was a fairly expensive item to begin with but this individual bought it for her father and had an electrician wire it properly to a switch on the wall by the curtained window.

They rigged it so two copper wires and copper strips were spaced far enough apart along the top of the railing where the seeds were so that none of the birds would be electrocuted when it was turned on. But because of his size the squirrel touched both wires and was a prime candidate for the electrical surprise.

The woman's father watched the first squirrel scampering along the railing picking up seed. So he walked to the switch and got ready. When he flipped the switch the squirrel instantly shot off into space, much to the glee of the viewers. Other squirrels were also sent airborne the same way but still they came back when no one was looking and helped themselves to the seed.

Only now the squirrels were more wary and paid attention to what was happening. Before long they saw the shadow of the old man as he moved to the window. They knew that was a sign that they were about to be launched. So they stayed away whenever they saw that someone was near the window. Finally the elderly gentleman was reduced to sneaking up on the window by crawling along the floor. But every time he peeked and was about to switch on for launch, the squirrels left before they got fired off into space. They had trained the man well. Squirrels don't like being peeked at.

Other people have been known to wire their bird feeder to the household electrical lines. It worked well and if they didn't burn down the feeder or the house the squirrels that received the jolt learned their lesson and never came back to that feeder again. They just moved next door to the neighbor's feeder that didn't give them that funny tingly feeling that fired them off into space.

Domes and gabled feeder roofs that stay in place by a single hole serve well to dump squirrel attackers from atop a feeder. I once installed baffles like a plastic garbage can lid to a post so they could not climb up it. Also the 1.5-liter plastic soda bottles strung on a line that goes from the neck out a hole in the bottom has gotten good reports. The squirrels try to balance themselves but invariably roll off sideways.

Another offbeat squirrel guard I have not seen working

but it comes highly recommended is the "Slinky." You may remember it as a toy from the past, the thing with the loose coils of wire that you could make slink from high places to lower places Well, one of those attached at the top so it hangs down around a support pole that squirrels have been climbing totally confuses the squirrels because the slinky coils always move when a squirrel tries to climb it.

To get some idea of how smart the enemy is in this war, watch this Youtube Video. It is one of the best ever made on this subject. Once you see how devilishly clever squirrels are you might want to retire from the field and come up with a different hobby.

https://m.youtube.com/watch?v=hFZFjoX2cGg

3 How to Build a Secret Weapon

I stumbled onto this idea of a squirrel safe birdfeeder because it was simple, inexpensive, and worked just fine. The key to whether or not it remains squirrel proof is where you hang it. As mentioned, mine went under the eaves of a small office building and was about 8 feet from the ground. Its gabled roof of galvanized metal with a hole in its middle provides rain protection and prevents squirrels trying to climb down from above. The feeder's roof tilts from their weight and they slide overboard. To fill it I lay it on the lawn and slide apart the parts on its central wire. Fill the coffee can with feed. When you pick it all up off the ground it comes together as shown in the sketch. Leave everything connected to its central hanging wire. You may need a stepladder to re-attach it to its hook under the eaves.

THINGS YOU WILL NEED

A wire cloths hanger.
A10-ounce empty coffee can with label and one end removed.
A standard aluminum pie pan.
And finally, the anti-squirrel device: a sheet of galvanized metal measuring 20x13.5 inches bent like a roof 4 inches down for the rain and squirrels to run off. Drill a 3/8-inch hole in the exact middle of that roof. To find it pencil lines to all 4 corners and where they cross hammer a nail point; then drill a 3/8th inch hole. *Voila,* your rust-proof, waterproof roof for your squirrel-free birdfeeder.

While you have the drill handy drill a 3/8-inch hole in the exact center of the bottom of your coffee can.

With your wire-cutters cut and straighten with your pliers that clothes hanger so you end up with the hook on the top end and the rest bent to form a straight wire all the way to its bottom end where once it is all assembled on the clothes hanger wire, you bend another small loop with your pliers to hold it all together when it is hung.

Now if you have your wild birdseed on hand you can assemble your bird feeder this way. Lay everything on your lawn and starting from the bottom put on the roof first sliding it up toward the hook. Next you punch three equal-spaced V-s around the edge of the open end of the coffee can, with a can punch punching them from the outside to the inside and removing the triangles of metal. Be careful of sharp edges. Thread this empty can bottom onto the wire. Drill a hole in the exact center of your pie pan slightly larger that the thickness of your coat hanger. This pan is the last item to thread onto the wire. With the pliers form the end into a loop so nothing will slip off. Now pick up the hook of your hanger and hold it up. All the parts of your feeder will come together. With the slack between the parts on the ground fill your coffee can with birdseed. Cover it with the pie pan and flip everything right side up holding it by its top hook. Hold the hook upright to kept it all together. Seed will come out the openings in the coffee can and the pie rim where birds will perch will keep it contained. Hang this feeder so that the pie pan is at least 6 feet above ground. Mine went on a strong hook screwed into the eaves of my office opposite its main window where my desk was. Squirrels trying to climb down by way of the feeder roof found it would tip them off. It also kept the seeds dry during rainstorms. Here's a sketch of how the feeder will look. The metal roof will rest on the bottom of the coffee can.

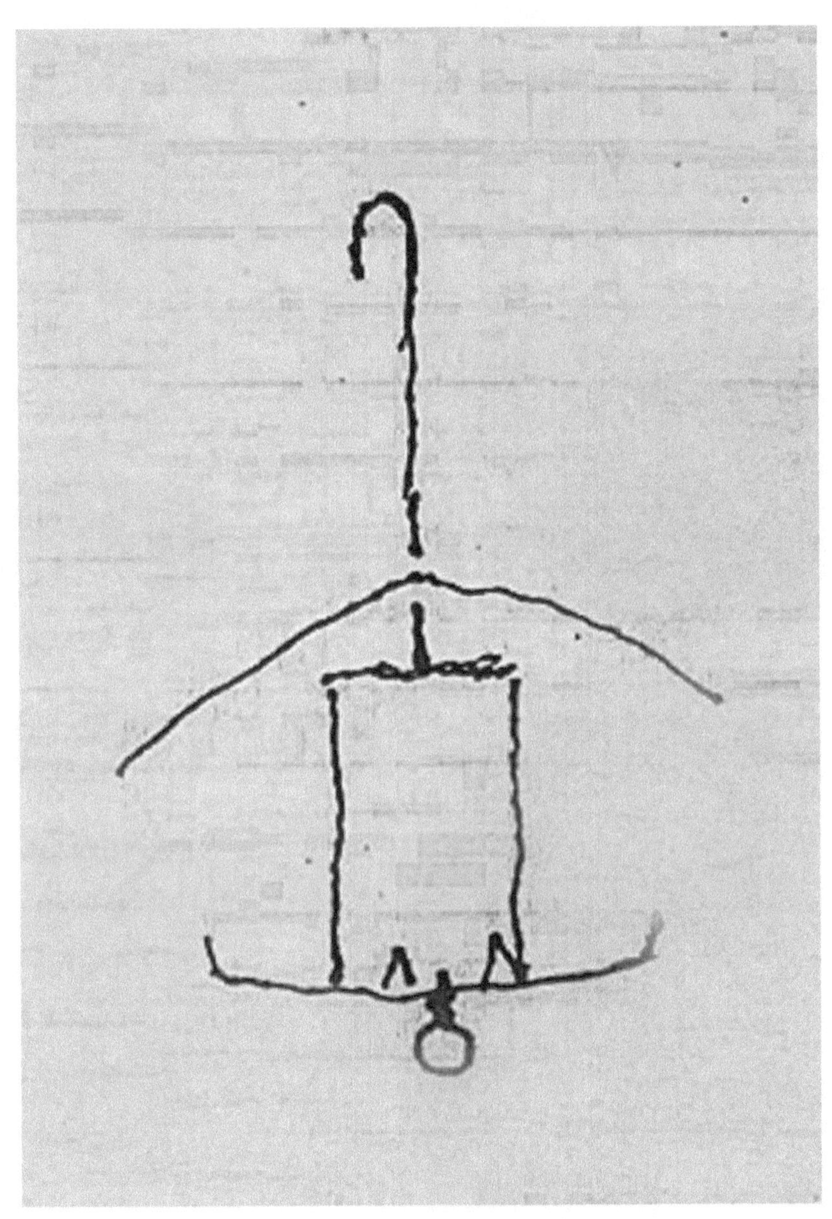

The roof rests upon the bottom of the coffee can.

4 Know Your Enemy

(Courtesy Wikipedia)

The Gray Squirrel

Squirrels may not like the idea of their family being classified as rodents but I'm afraid that is what he is right along with the rats and mice of our world. As far as I'm concerned I attach no stigma to either rats or mice since as a kid I raised and enjoyed both kinds – a big albino white rat named Larry and an always-growing family of white mice. They all looked alike so they never got named. Since they were very prolific my Mom made me give the entire family away to other friends that wanted Mickey Mouse pets with pink eyes. Larry stayed with me for years and was very affectionate.

Here are more specifics on this fellow we sometimes call a cat squirrel in the Deep South but who in fact is more formally known as an Eastern Gray Squirrel.

Eastern Gray Squirrel

Rodent

Description

The eastern gray squirrel, also known as the grey squirrel depending on region, is a tree squirrel in the genus *Sciurus*. It is native to eastern North America, where it is the most prodigious and ecologically essential natural forest regenerator.

Scientific name: *Sciurus carolinensis*

Mass: 0.88 – 1.3 lbs (Adult)
Gestation period: 44 days
Length: 9.1 – 12 in. (Adult, Head and body)
Conservation status: Least Concern (Population increasing)
Encyclopedia of Life

Like many members of the family *Sciuridae*, the eastern gray
squirrel is a scatter-hoarder; it hoards food in numerous small
caches for later recovery. Some caches are quite temporary,
especially those made near the site of a sudden abundance of
food which can be retrieved within hours or days for reburial
in a more secure site. Others are more permanent and are not
retrieved until months later. Each squirrel is estimated to
make several thousand caches each season. The squirrels have
very accurate spatial memory for the locations of these caches,
and use distant and nearby landmarks to retrieve them. Smell
is used partly to uncover food caches, and also to find food in
other squirrels' caches. Scent can be unreliable when the
ground is too dry or covered in snow.[19]

Squirrels sometimes use deceptive behavior to prevent other
animals from retrieving cached food.

[Stop and think about how clever the following is because it
typifies the kind of sneaky devilish thinking we birdfeeder
protectors are up against!] **They will pretend to bury the
object if they feel that they are being watched.** They do this
by preparing the spot as usual, for instance, digging a hole or
widening a crack, miming the placement of the food, while
actually concealing it in their mouths, and then covering up
the "cache" as if they had deposited the object. They also hide
behind vegetation while burying food or hide it high up in
trees (if their rival is not a tree-lover). I have seen one sneakily
recovering seeds on the ground by covering his entire head
and body with a fuzzy tail that blended him right in with the
ground cover. You could look right at him and not be sure it

wasn't a curled dead leaf! These squirrels possess a complex repertoire of similar behaviors that they are not borne with. Such a complex collection of devious ploys can only be the products of a thinking mind. In this case that scrounging squirrel knew I was watching him from about 20 feet away so he was hiding in plain sight under that flared out bushy tail!

The eastern gray squirrel is one of very few mammalian species that can descend a tree headfirst. It does this by turning its feet so the claws of its hind paws are backward pointing and can grip the tree bark.

Eastern gray squirrels build a type of nest, known as a drey, in the forks of trees, consisting mainly of dry leaves and twigs. The dreys are roughly spherical, about 30 to 60 cm in diameter and are usually insulated with moss, thistledown, dried grass, and feathers to reduce heat loss. Males and females may share the same nest for short times during the breeding season, and during cold winter spells. Squirrels may share a drey to stay warm. They may also nest in the attic or exterior walls of a house, where they may be regarded as pests, as well as fire hazards due to their habit of gnawing on electrical cables. In addition, squirrels may inhabit a permanent tree den hollowed out in the trunk or a large branch of a tree. When I saw a Gray squirrel stealthily disappear under the eaves of a small office building beside my house I checked to see where he went. The squirrels had gnawed their way through the eaves and were exploring my sealed off office attic. Once their exploring was over and they were gone, I nailed and sealed a wooden cover over that hole. So far it has remained sealed. But we have all heard tales about squirrels that have invaded attics to raise their young. If this happens it's time to call in the trained professional to get rid of them as quickly as possible.

I once had a gray squirrel fall down my fireplace chimney. He ended up scratching and making a racket behind the ceramic heating grates of the gas fireplace in my living room. I sealed all other living room exits and opened wide my front door. Then I eased the fireplace forward. Out popped a very sooty, very frightened black squirrel that took one look at me then ricocheted around my living room leaving black smudges wherever he hit the walls until he found the open front door and shot through it. I have no idea whether he accidentally fell down the chimney or was pushed but it gave him a great story to tell. Fortunately it never happened again.

Eastern gray squirrels are more active during the early and late hours of the day, and tend to avoid the heat in the middle of a summer day. They do not hibernate. For a week or more in mid-summer mine could almost always attack the bird feeder at 10 A.M., when the birds seemed most anxious to feed. Usually I was up at dawn to fill the feeder but seldom saw more than a single lonely cardinal looking for that early worm.

Of course once the squirrels launched one of their swift hit and run attacks the birds all sat in nearby trees watching us fight it out with shouted words and squirrel chatter while me and the attackers yelled at each other. I swear I think the birds were not annoyed but were more entertained by it all.

Once the commotion ceased they went back to feeding again. A couple hours latter the war started again and the birds took another break and repeated what they usually did until the broo-ha-ha was over. Then they returned to the feeder and picked up where they left off.

Eastern gray squirrels can breed twice a year, but younger and less experienced mothers normally have a single litter per year in the spring. Depending on forage availability, older and more experienced females may breed again in summer. In a year of abundant food, 36% of females bear two litters, but none will do so in a year of poor food. Their breeding seasons are December to February and May to June, though this is slightly delayed in more northern latitudes. The first litter is born in February or March, the second in June or July, though, again, bearing may be advanced or delayed by a few weeks depending on climate, temperature, and forage availability. In any given breeding season, an average of 61-66% of females bear young. If a female fails to conceive or loses her young to unusually cold weather or predation, she re-enters estrus and has a later litter. Five days before a female enters estrus, she may attract up to 34 males from up to 500 meters away. Eastern gray squirrels exhibit a form of polygamy, in which the competing males will form a hierarchy of dominance, and the female will mate with multiple males depending on the hierarchy established.

Normally, one to four young are born in each litter, but the largest possible litter size is eight. The gestation period is about 44 days. The young are weaned around 10 weeks, though some may wean up to six weeks later in the wild. They begin to leave the nest after 12 weeks, with autumn born young often wintering with their mother. Only one in four squirrel kits survives to one year of age, with mortality around 55% for the following year. Mortality rates then decrease to around 30% for following years until they increase sharply at eight years of age.

These squirrels can live to be 20 years old in captivity, but in the wild they live much shorter lives due to predation and the challenges of their habitat. At birth, their life expectancy is 1-2 years; an adult typically can live to be six, with exceptional individuals making it to 12 years.

Newborn gray squirrels weigh 13-18 grams and are entirely hairless and pink. Full adult body mass is achieved by 8-9 months after birth.

Communication

As in most other mammals, communication among eastern gray squirrel individuals involves both vocalizations and posturing. The species has quite a varied repertoire of vocalizations, including a squeak similar to that of a mouse, a low-pitched noise, a chatter, and a raspy "mehr mehr mehr". Other methods of communication include tail-flicking and other gestures, including facial expressions. Tail flicking and the "kuk" or "quaa" call are used to ward off and warn other squirrels about predators, as well as to announce when a predator is leaving the area. Squirrels also make an affectionate coo-purring sound that biologists call the "muk-muk" sound. This is used as a contact sound between a mother and her kits and in adulthood, by the male when he courts the female during mating season.

After a fairly successful raid on my feeder, my friend and I have heard them perhaps discussing their raid in the thickets. The sound is one we would not associate with squirrels. Not the usual chatter they make upon seeing an approaching dog perhaps. But these are varied vocalizations one might hear people making as they sit on a front porch and talk together. Sometimes the squirrels sound as though they are laughing at us and I suspect they are. Of course after I've turned the air blue behind their escape they may be hurling similar insults over their shoulders as they make off with the bulk of the loot.

Those who study such things say that their use of vocal and visual communication has been shown to vary by location, based on elements such as noise pollution and the amount of open space. For instance, populations living in large cities generally rely more on the visual signals, due to the generally louder environment with more areas without much visual restriction. However, in heavily wooded areas, vocal signals are used more often due to the relatively lower noise levels and a dense canopy restricting visual range.

The latter is certainly true about our rural area. The one time I notice they make no sounds at all is when they are trying to get away with something. For instance if I see a squirrel making a bee-line for the right side of my backyard he does it with strong leaps as he bounds across. Nothing squirrelly ever happens on the right side of my yard so I am always puzzled when I see them tearing up the grass to get to the opposite side. They know where I sit and that I am watching, but I have never figured out why they race across all that open space. It's not like I have my howitzers set up to take pot shots at them as they cross. But equally mysterious is when they come back to the thickets on the left side of the yard. They do it very covertly, not with a hop but what I would call more a crawl on all fours crouching low in the grass and going slow as though I can't see them. Beats me why, but I hold my fire and just watch their stealthy tactics through my binoculars. I suspect they are planning something or other but so far I haven't figured out what it is. Recently I've noticed one or two of them taking interest in my large boatshed of sailboats in my backyard that shelters a fiberglass dinghy, along with a couple kayaks, a skiff, two live-aboard sailboats, a Hobi Cat, a fiberglass canoe and a see-through wood and Lucite dinghy. The latter once supported a grass squirrel nest far back under the seats. I'll have to keep an eye on things out there.

Diet

Without a doubt squirrels possess a set of teeth that can gnaw through virtually anything they care to gnaw through. My small white office building beside the house appears to be sheathed on the outside with bulletin board covered by a hard plastic coat of something the squirrels decided they liked. I would be inside and they started gnawing the outside. It sounded as though I was inside a huge bass drum and someone was scratching the outside with a steel file. When I rushed outside and turned the air blue the noise-makes scrambled to get away and the neighborhood dogs barked excitedly again.

In time the squirrels gnawed all the surface coating off in some places as though it had been sanded. Maybe they were chalk hungry. I hastily painted back all the places with white Latex paint and they stopped their gnawing. Maybe it provided something they lacked in their diet. Maybe they were just sharpening their teeth. Maybe they were just doing it to fire me up. I never learned what it was so it remains a mystery,

Hard-as-nails-shells of Hickory nuts and Hazelnuts gnawed by gray squirrels show a curved pattern of cut marks left by their sharp incisors that look like miniature scooped ice cream grooves. The only other things I know that makes that kind of groove in those shells are diamond tipped drills.

Another part of the squirrel's anatomy that is remarkable is their digestive system.
They eat many things they find in their environment…nuts, bark, green sprouts and seeds hidden within a green pinecone. Many kinds of fruits and berries are squirrel food. During World War two in northern Italy after the shooting stopped markets featured lots of tiny birds as pets. But I bought a squirrel mainly so I could let him go. I had never seen an Italian squirrel up close and mine like all the others there had tufted ears. For a few days with us he lived in a cage on our windowsill where the only food I remember him eating with gusto were apples. After the squad enjoyed him for a while I let him go so he could do whatever Italian squirrels with tufted ears do on a nice day in the springtime. It is doubtful anyone had a birdfeeder going in those days but there were always plenty of acorns available where we were stationed.

The reason I mentioned their cast-iron constitution is because squirrels can eat things that would poison us. One of them is the early spring production of fruit produced by the Chinaberry trees in our area. For a long time I wondered at their acrobatics at the very end of a heavily leafed-out limb as they swished back and forth getting the tender green nibblets each spring, When I glassed the limb 40 feet overhead I saw the lance-shaped leaves and found a picture online.

**Chinaberries are poisonous to man,
but not to squirrels.**

Scientists say that squirrels eat a wide variety of foods, such as tree bark, tree buds, berries, many types of seeds and acorns, walnuts, and other nuts, like hazelnuts and some types of fungi found in the forests, including fly agaric mushrooms (*Amanita muscaria*). Squirrels can cause damage to trees by tearing the bark and eating the soft cambial tissue underneath. In Europe, sycamore (*Acer pseudoplatanus* L.) and beech (*Fagus sylvatica* L.) suffer the greatest damage. The squirrels also raid gardens for tomatoes, corn, strawberries, and other garden crops, much I'm sure to the annoyance of farmers who probably immediately think of hooking the varmints up to a deer zapper. Sometimes they eat the tomato seeds and discard the rest. On occasion, eastern gray squirrels also prey upon insects, frogs, small rodents including other squirrels, and small birds, their eggs, and young. They also gnaw on bones, antlers, and turtle shells – likely as a source of minerals scarce in their normal diet.

Eastern gray squirrels have a high enough tolerance for humans to inhabit residential neighborhoods and raid bird feeders for millet, corn, and sunflower seeds. Some people who feed and watch birds for entertainment also intentionally feed seeds and nuts to the squirrels for the same reason.

There is at least one incident on record in which a family was proud of the fact that they could entice wild squirrels right into their house and feed them by hand. Once the squirrels learned where their food supplies were kept, that was all they needed to know. When the family left for a few days vacation they came back to find the inside of their house reduced to shambles after the squirrels gnawed a hole through their back door looking for their usual handout.

It is reported that in the UK eastern gray squirrels can eat a tremendous amount of food from birdfeeders and thereby prevent the local wild birds from getting any. This has resulted in a reduction in the population of wild birds. Attraction to supplementary feeders can increase local bird nest predation, as eastern gray squirrels are more likely to forage near feeders, resulting in increased likelihood of finding nests and eating the eggs. All of which is difficult for me to imagine since I have never seen or heard of our southern squirrels involved in this kind of predation.

In the wild, eastern gray squirrels can be found inhabiting large areas of mature, dense woodland ecosystems, generally covering 100 acres (40 hectares) of land. These forests usually contain large mast-producing trees [meaning nut-producing] such as oaks and hickories, providing ample food sources. Through The South in the USA that primarily includes pine trees and their freshly produced pine cones that are highly prized by our population of squirrels. Oak-hickory hardwood forests are generally preferred over coniferous forests due to the greater abundance of mast forage. This is why they are found only in parts of eastern Canada that do not contain boreal forest (i.e. they are found in some parts of New Brunswick, in southwestern Quebec, throughout southern Ontario and in southern Manitoba).

Eastern gray squirrels generally prefer constructing their dens upon large tree branches and within the hollow trunks of trees. They also have been known to take shelter within abandoned bird nests. The dens are usually lined with moss plants, thistledown, dried grass, and feathers. These perhaps provide and assist in the insulation of the den, used to reduce heat loss. A cover to the den is usually built afterwards.

Close to human settlements, eastern gray squirrels are found in parks and back yards of houses within urban environments and in the farmlands of rural environments.

It has become the most common squirrel in many urban and suburban habitats in western North America, from north of central California to southwest British Columbia. At the turn of the 20th century, the eastern gray squirrel was introduced into South Africa, Ireland, Hawaii, Bermuda, Madeira Island, the Azores, the Canary Islands, Cape Verde, Italy and the United Kingdom.

Gray squirrels were eaten in earlier times by Native

Americans and their meat is still popular with hunters across most of their range in North America. Growing up in a hunter/fisherman family we included squirrels in our hunt for game that included rabbits, pheasants, quail and partridges. Since I made my living for many years writing about hunting and fishing for the outdoor magazines, one of my most interesting features for *Outdoor Life* one year was how we had to hunt from a boat in an incredibly dense tropical jungle in north Florida because the vegetation was so thick the game heard us moving and disappeared. For three days three of us lived on swamp cabbage [palmetto trunks] and fried squirrels in a wild piece of Eden where we heard a Florida panther scream at night. The feature was titled **The Spooky Grays of Tate's Hell**.

Now, back to the war that so many of us have with these birdseed raiders. First however is how it all began in my area of the South and how I managed to resolve it peaceably to the point where the squirrels are content, the birds at their feeder are happy and I no longer frighten them with my shouts. Even the neighborhood dogs seldom rouse themselves to bark the neighborhood is so peaceful now. Here's how it all came about.

5 My Squirrel War History

Many years ago I bought my first bird feeder because it was such an unusual idea. It was a 7-inch diameter clear plastic cylinder about 4 inches deep. Suction cups on the back of it attached it to a window outdoors. The feeder's back was a one-way mirror. The circular front had its upper half cut out. Seed went into the bottom half and the birds perched on that cut away half of the front panel. The mirrored back enabled birds to see their reflections but being one-way they did not see the bird-lovers watching them through the window from inside the house just inches away from them. As I recall it usually attracted two birds at a time and there was some quarreling among them every day as to which two birds got there before the others.

The best feature about this feeder was that the birds had no idea that people watched them. The kids loved it because they could put their faces up to the window just inches from the eager feeders. Squirrels never bothered the feeder because it was virtually un-reachable for them. The bad part was that it handled only a couple feathered friends at a time.

This probably is the reason I decided to build a feeder that would take care of all the birds at the same time. We had two sets of wide Jalousie windows that went across the family room/kitchen facing to the west. A davenport in front of the windows with its back to the windows was for our family of birdwatchers..

Without even a thought about squirrels I built a bird feeder extending for 5 feet across part of that wide set of windows. Four 2-inch diameter PVC pipes driven into the ground at windowsill level supported the large wooden frame whose underside was covered with screen-door screen so rain would run through it.

A large amount of mixed birdseed went into that tray and for about three days every bird in the neighborhood worked it over heavily. After that the squirrels discovered it and from then on it was no longer a birdfeeder but a squirrel feeder. My war with squirrels began on that day.

These gray squirrels had to learn that they should not scare all my bird friends away while they gobbled up the goodies. But these were not the big old Fox squirrels that I grew up with. A Fox squirrel species lived in Florida all right but seemed not to be as prominent as they were up North, in fact along one of our roads to a Federal Park you almost always saw members of a Fox squirrel family that were white albinos in that area.

Those in our yard however, were the much smaller Northwest Florida Gray Squirrels. This bushy-tailed member of the rodent family has grayish-brown fur with paler fur on their undersides. The tail often has silvery-tipped hairs at the end. Eastern gray squirrels can grow 17 to 20 inches long. Florida is home to two other species of squirrels, the fox squirrel (*Sciurus niger*) and the southern flying squirrel (*Glaucomys volans*).

Eastern gray squirrels occur in woodland and urban areas, especially near oaks and hickories, and are active during the day, often feeding on the ground. They spend much of their lives in trees.

The eastern gray squirrel hoards food in numerous places for later recovery. They have the ability to recall the location of thousands of food caches. Preferred foods include bark, berries, seeds and acorns. North Florida is renown for its large forests of long-leaf pine grown especially for the paper industry. Squirrels love the early growth of pine cones. Though prickly to handle and hard as a rock, squirrels cut them off early and peel back the tightly packed prongs to get at the tender sweet inner parts called *mast* that they like.

Here is one observer's account of that: "I've observed red squirrels biting off white pine cones, which land with a "thump" about every ten seconds. When watching a squirrel forage amid Norway spruce, I saw it carry away cones almost as long as its 7-inch body. Most cones are cached in the shade of mature conifers – hoarded for the winter either individually or in mounds called *middens* that are secreted underground, beneath rocks, or in a hollow tree. A red squirrel's acute sense of smell can detect seed caches buried under a foot of soil and beneath snow up to 12 feet deep.

The squirrels usually balance the green cone on a limb to eat; chewing scales off the core of a cone the way people eat corn-on-the-cob. First, it chews the scales off near the stem. As each scale falls away, a pair of seeds is exposed. Because seeds grow in a spiral, the squirrel has to turn the cone as he eats. Mounds of discarded scales and naked cone-cores pile up wherever a squirrel partakes of its pine-on-the-cob.

Squirrels peel cones for their tender seeds.

Dropped cones and cores litter the ground.

Most of the dropped cones show the squirrel lost them at their cutting, These are heavy, sharply pointed very prickly projectiles that thud to the ground with a sound that tells you that coming from that distance it would surely do serious damage to anyone's head if the two came together.

As for my tray birdfeeder, it soon became apparent that if my birds were going to have a chance at this smorgasbord, something had to be done about the pesky squirrels. My neighbor's teenage son offered to help with his CO_2 propelled pellet handgun swearing that it was not lethal but would only sting the squirrels.

The one shot he took missed and put a neat round BB hole in my wife's bedroom window. That was the end of the BB gun effort.

I found a friend who offered me loan of his live catch trap. It worked fine. But each time I caught a squirrel I had to drive several miles outside of town to the release him in a Federal Park. I made that trip so many times that I swear there was always a welcoming committee of squirrels every time I let a squirrel go free. The entire squirrel family always turned out to welcome a new arrival.

That got tiresome in a hurry. I finally took down the free food tray and put up a couple long tall columns of feeders with perches and holes over their full length. The squirrels loved them. They wrapped themselves around them and once they got a forepaw into a hole it all started going into their mouths. I put barbed wire around the seed holes. This only slowed the process. Finally I retired those feeders.

Next I bought what I considered was a standard birdfeeder. It was six-sided and all plastic with a peaked roof. A knob on top fitted into an internal slot and locked it all together. Undoing that knob and lifting the roof enabled me to fill it. My seed measure provided about two cups of seed that seemed to satisfy what our local birds wanted.

I mounted the feeder on a shepherd's hook, one-inch thick solid black rod with a side rest for my foot when I stepped on it to drive it into the ground. Its curved arms put the feeder about 6 feet above the ground. I drilled a hole in the feeder's bottom and inserted a wood peg that contained a hook. Under the feeder I hung wind chimes. The idea being that each morning when I replenished the birdseed, the sound of the disturbed wind chimes would call the birds to come get their breakfast. It worked great. Soon, all the neighborhood birds were conditioned to come when the chimes rang. Unfortunately, the squirrels got conditioned to come too. Hanging from the other arm was my Humming bird feeder. It too was popular with a pair of thirsty hummers.

Hummer is glad no one wants his food.

Since it was exposed to inclement weather, rain made a mess of the birdseed so I topped this feeder with the roof of my unused homemade feeder; that sheet of galvanized metal was bent at an angle so that it shielded the feeder and the birds stayed dry for breakfast in the rain. A hole in the roof's center for the feeder's suspension wire enabled it to be a shifty proposition for any squirrel trying to approach from the top; so it served two purposes.

Remarkably I had no squirrel problem for a long time with this arrangement. But one day when I looked at the feeder I saw that something on top of it was under that roof resting in its shade. Looking closer I found an Oak snake hoping to have breakfast there with the birds. I carefully let him slither onto a broom handle and took him across the street into the woods where I'm sure he was a lot happier.

Eventually the family of gray squirrels living nearby in the thickets and trees developed a taste for birdseed. I often had to run them off the feeder where I think they would have liked to take up permanent residence.

Since they were climbing that one-inch thick rod, I made it a bit more fun for them by slathering it with Vaseline. Watching the squirrels "spinning their wheels" so to speak was quite a spectacle until the stuff dried in the sun and was no longer slippery.

In the meantime the squirrels learned to do a standing broad-jump that usually let them grab wind chimes and hold onto something so they could clamor the rest of the onto the birdfeeder and have their way with it.

To counter that I shortened the suspension lines for the feeder and got rid of the chimes because the squirrels leaned they could climb up through those pipes and strings no matter how much racket they made.

I hung the feeder higher and got rid of their handy rod-climbing ability by surrounding that rod with a tall 10-inch wide PVC pipe painted to match the background greenery.

This worked well for a period of time until the squirrels began leaping like big bullfrogs and somehow managed to get back on that feeder. I added a PVC extension and hoisted the feeder higher. Still they outsmarted me.

After looking at all of the anti-squirrel feeders I decided to stick with my original one and somehow hang it where the squirrels could not leap up to it.

The 12-foot high carport ceiling looked like it might work.

All the bird action could be easily seen from my table and chairs and a dozen juniper Bonsais I had scattered around me there. Besides it was a natural breezeway and a comfortable place to read. So I came up with this idea for the open end of this carport:

In the middle of the carport eaves where the carport overhang protects it from rain I screwed in an eyebolt to take a small pulley. At the top of the support pipe I tied a line for another pulley. The line attached to the wire cable supporting the feeder was than run through that pulley and down to the ground. Here are pictures of this arrangement:

Getting seed out of supply.

Lowering feeder.

Feeder is filled through its roof.

Shaking fills the tray.

Easy hitch secures the hoisted feeder.

Ready for customers; squirrel baffle in place.

Three colorful characters enjoying their lunch.

I have read accounts where others have had Fox squirrels
literally gnaw through a clothesline support of the feeder
sending it crashing to smithereens so the squirrels get all they
can eat.

This may occur with larger more determined squirrels.
But I find the smaller gray squirrels common to the South are
far less aggressive. Not one of them managing to raid my
carport feeder ever realized I never lock down the roof of the
feeder because it is easier to fill without that. If Our Gang of
raiders ever realized that, they would have that top off in an
instant and surely one of them – probably Spanky the smallest
and youngest – would be ordered inside the feeder to speed
up the dispersal of goodies. Since my feeder is many years old
I recently looked to see what contemporary designs were
available at Wal-Mart. To my surprise their feeder appeared to
be a modern day copy of mine. It too was six sided which
meant the food openings were small well placed and
economical in how much feed came through for the birds.
However the plastic sides were round and the roof looked six-
sided and identical except that the plastic nut on top did not
move and was part of the roof. Nothing locked down the roof.
You merely lifted up the wire suspension cable to pour in the
feed. You can dismantle it this way for cleaning. All told it
would be my choice if I needed another one. Priced at $9.95 it
was practically what I had that was still working well.

As we moved through our summer months this
combination of carport birdfeeder seemed to be the best
combo I could think of to deter the squirrels. What I had
created was a small obstacle course to my feeder. Naturally
they quickly went to work on how to get around my obstacles.
Without their being aware of it I watched them as they
checked it out, looking for weaknesses in my defense. Every
time one of them went up the pole I heard from my detector
so I stealthily spied on the intruder's progress.

The black pipes supporting the carport roof were easy for

them to climb. But at the top they had to get onto the clothesline and walk its tightrope distance of five feet to reach the next pulley down to the suspended feeder.

Someone said that Pam, the cooking spray, made a nice slippery surface for squirrels. So I pammed the pole they climbed and watched their sliding frustrations. The line along the pole helped give the climber something to hold onto. When the squirrel finally reached the top he had to go onto the tightrope and balance his way to the distant prize. So I put a baffle there to stop him. It was a large tinfoil pie pan. If a squirrel put weight on the pan it revolved. I threaded the line through a hole in its bottom. Of course that stopped them only for a day. I watched as this turned the squirrels away several times. But then they found they could push the pan ahead of them as they crawled that tightrope until they reached the prize.

When I returned home after being away all morning that pie pan baffle had been pushed to the down-line to the feeder and it was well cleaned out.

So to stop this I put an overhand knot in the rope so it stopped the pan from being pushed by the squirrel to the feeder. The squirrels simply pushed harder and made a larger hole. Then they bypassed the knot and pushed the pan to the down-line.

I pushed the pan back to the beginning and clamped on a small pair of locking pliers that stopped that nonsense at once. But any peaceful solution with my local squirrels seemed impossible. They were determined to raid the birdfeeder no matter how hard I tried to stop them.

In the seven months we waged war, one incident – which was the opening attack I described at the beginning of this book – brought about a comment from a friend that made me see this conflict from an entirely different angle. After I e-mailed her my description of the chaotic attack with my yelling and a description of the ricocheting squirrels and my wondering what the neighbors thought about this entire disturbance she responded with this e-mail:

"I'm sure you gave your neighbors a surprise or they might be used to it. Lol
Poor little squirrel...it's so hungry.
We have some aggravating ones here too. They eat our pecans...a lot!
See you tomorrow."
What?
"Poor little squirrel...it's so hungry!"

I hadn't even thought about that! All I saw were squirrels stealing food from my song birds, scaring them away so they could get it all.

But her remark made me think about it in a totally different way. Could it be true? *Were the squirrels really doing it from hunger*?

What other reasons could there be I asked myself. Spite? Because they could? Because they are smarter than we mere Men?

The last thoughts were doubtful but this was War! And war is hell! We were up against a very clever enemy. I admit, most of us don't like being out-smarted by a toothy, grinning rodent! So we fight back tooth and nail against him. Me with my noisy bluster because it worked. It scared hell out of the Enemy.

So does that make you a victor? asked a small voice in my conscience.

Well, in a war where you can't use slings and arrows it's a pretty good second, my conscience answered itself. Always scares hell out of them and the neighborhood dogs. Seems that's at least a small hint of victory!

My problem with squirrels always was because they kept the birds away so they could steal most of the bird feed. The reason I was so angry was because I saw this as an act of aggression against the birds. They had done nothing to irritate the squirrels. But the squirrels had rushed in and were aggressively stealing the food placed there for the birds.

Was I wrong in seeing it that way? I thought that most men would see it that way too and see the squirrels as the aggressors stealing food from the helpless birds.

But this is the kind of thinking that perpetuates the Squirrel War. What always made it more contentious was the fact that the smart little aggressors almost always outsmarted us men who constantly tried to outsmart them. So the war perpetuated itself.

When I e-mailed my friend describing the squirrel attack as I did in detail, I expected that she would e-mail back a sympathetic response for me the protector of all birds and enemy of all seed-stealing squirrels.

But no. She responded the way a women was much more likely to respond, going deeper than a man might go and feeling sympathy for "the poor little hungry squirrel."

To me that seemed like a much more logical feminine way to think. I realize many women would be appalled to hear about such aggressive efforts to steal something. But this woman who comes from a large family of children and grandchildren simply replied to my e-mail with her honest motherly feeling that to me went beyond the obvious aggression to steal. Her thinking went deeper than mine when she wrote:

"That poor hungry little squirrel."

As I said earlier, this was the first time I realized I had never thought about that. Never asked myself **why** were they so determined to get that food?

For the first time I now thought maybe it was because they were desperate, that they indeed were hungry. Where hunger is concerned there are no limits to what man or beast will do to provide for themselves and their family.

That thought instantly provided me with a possible way to resolve the problem and our war if the squirrels would accept it. I knew they already had learned to forage with the larger birds in the area where I was throwing a handful of seed, broadcasting it over the right side of our lawn.

A lone squirrel searches the lawn where
feed for big birds is scattered.

Once they started doing that I encouraged it with more birdseed. What I liked to see was the whole squirrel family going there first to look with the doves and larger birds. I liked that the squirrels eagerly worked like the others to find that seed. So I increased the amounts I threw out there for them. More seeds encouraged them to hunt for food rather than steal it. Now they became competitive with the other bottom feeders. If the squirrels were satisfied with that, it put them all on the same level and left the birdfeeder seeds high above them for the smaller birds.

Also, later in the afternoon one by one the entire squirrel family came and enjoyed the fall-out seeds under the feeders. Not a great amount since most of it was sunflower shells but the best part was that squirrels were finding enough food there to keep them interested. And best of all, eight feet overhead where the source was, they acted as if the birdfeeder wasn't even there!

Easily had spillover seeds keeps the squirrel's mind off the overhead birdfeeder.

Seeds for the eating beats fighting for them.

Lots of blackbirds help the cleanup.

This pleased me enormously. For the first time ever, the squirrels were working to find their food. As long as they did it peaceably I supplied more for them on the ground. It worked like magic.

Then finally came the day when the first swishing sound and then solid thud told me that the squirrels were now starting to enjoy their harvest of green pine cones in our yard. That "Whomp" was one that slipped out of their grasp as they balanced the heavy thing on a branch and tried to peel it back to the tender green edibles they found inside.

I was glad to see that other things were adding to their choice of foods. But I continued with the birdfeed in the yard, giving them that choice that they could get easy by just looking for it. Those handfuls I broadcasted across one side of my lawn seemed interesting enough to encourage both birds and squirrels to compete in looking for it. Also, on the concrete underneath the birdfeeder was a lot of seed that normally got knocked out and the same thing was happening. Now, both squirrels and birds were always picking at the seeds scattered across the concrete.

Once a week I took the leaf blower and blew all of it out into my lawn. They all had a good time working for what they got.

And the best part was that they left the main feeder for the flying birds. The birds at the feeder did their bit by scattering the goodies. Most of the cardinals behaved themselves and there were a lot of them. The young birds that was almost as large as the parents came with them. Often the youngster sat by himself off to one side. A television satellite dish on the lawn was often a good spot. The parent, usually the female, would get a sunflower seed at the feeder, crack it and carry it to the youngster.

She did this repeatedly; then flew off and the youngster followed. The way you could always tell which one was the youngster was by watching his behavior.

Every time his mother would look at him he would puff out his feathers and shiver, his wings trembling as if he was suffering so badly from hunger she couldn't get it to him fast enough. Other times she would stay at the feeder with him right beside her, trembling up a storm and she ignored him. Usually she would fly off leaving him setting there.

As long as she was not there, he never trembled. Once in a while he might get a seed for himself. One can only guess that she was weaning him off his dependency on her for food. The oddball among my birdfeeders was a red-headed woodpecker. His size alone indicated that he was too big for this feeder but he repeatedly proved me wrong. He was a contortionist and an acrobat. When he came in for a fast seed he would grab the rail with his feet and layback, upside down, then stretch his long neck and slide his long bill into the feeding trough. In an instant he grabbed a sunflower seed, then let go of his perch as he dropped and rolled and winged off with his prize. It was always a sight to see. Here he is in action.

Woodpecker acrobatics.

Once I realized that the squirrels were willing to look for
scattered birdseed in the grass, my feelings for them changed.
Their raids to the birdfeeder stopped instantly. Instead of
being mad at the squirrels for outsmarting me, I began to feel
that I was the real winner of our war with each other. We
became friends. I admired how all four squirrels worked to
get what they wanted, which was simply something to eat. I
got a kick out of how they kept track of me. If I was out sitting
under the carport, they almost always came and got a drink
out of the birdbath I had moved there. I talked to them in a
low voice. They listened. Sometimes I caught them quite close,
feeding on seeds that had blown closer to my chair. Whenever
I moved, I had to move the way our Vietnam War snipers
moved when in the bush. Extremely slow. Otherwise anything
like a normal movement sent them rocketing for cover.

If they went bounding across my yard for the trees and
cover on the east side of the yard where the big birds searched
for seed in the grass, I was always amazed to see them
sometimes going back the other way, but this time not
hopping and running but moving slowly through the grass on
all fours the way a squirrel would that thinks he is invisible. I
used a miniature pair of binoculars to study their movements
in detail. These were 8x21 Bushnell lens glasses chosen
especially because they could be close-focused less that 20 feet
when I watched them on the feeder. I always kept the squirt
gun loaded and ready because it had a range of about 20 feet.
But instead of a defensive weapon I found that the squirrels
loved it. One day Spanky was sneaking back and forth across
the long grass on some kind of secret mission of his own. To
let him know that I had my eye on him I picked up the squirt
gun and let him have it. He stopped, curled his widely spread
tail over his back and stayed right there enjoying his
refreshing shower. So much for warding off a squirrel attack
with a squirt gun.

My feeling for the squirrels had changed radically from

the way I thought about them when they were stealing my birdseed. It made me think of something that happened to my Grandpa when I was a little kid. I used to row for him when he fished for an old enemy of his. It was a big, smart old fish that always got away from him. He was a giant pickerel Grandpa named Toby. Remembering Grandpa and Toby helped me understand how I felt about squirrels. I had been at war with them. Grandpa Joe had been at War with Toby. But at the end of their lives they were no longer enemies. They made peace and I knew how they did it. I could see it happening to the squirrels and me. In both incidences there is a word for it. I wrote about them many years ago. Here's that story:

6 How Grandpa Fought the Good Fight

Originally titled Uncle Josh and the Lake Monster, *this story was my first published fishing article. It appeared in the* Florida Wildlife Magazine. *Only the names are fictional. Uncle Josh was my Grandpa Joe Brown who owned a barbershop in Grand Rapids, Michigan. The fish, a giant pickerel, was really called Toby, not Ned. It actually happened at Spring Lake, Michigan. I was about nine or ten years old at the time and always rowed the large green rowboat while Grandpa trolled for Toby. The two of them had been feuding off and on for years. Grandpa always lost the big fish for some reason or other. Usually Toby broke his line. We would motor under the bridge and into Smith's Bayou where the big fish hung out. It was a strange place with lots of marl bottom. In retrospect I guess this is my freshwater version of "The Old Man and the Sea." I was with Hemingway in Pamplona in 1959. I wonder what he would have thought of my story. Times were hard in my grandfather's day. Our families were hunters and fishermen. Here's a photograph of Grandpa Joe and me with our rabbit hunting hounds.*

With Grandpa Joe and our hunting
hounds Pal and Lindy.

Uncle Josh and the Lake Monster

THE CYPRESS-RIMMED lake lay shimmering under the first playful shafts of morning sun. A hungry bass rose for a Harvest Fly, belly-whacked the surface and disappeared beneath a cascade of quicksilver. Sitting on the front steps of his cottage, Uncle Josh calmly ignored the invitation and thoughtfully ran his fingers through his white hair. There was an unusual restlessness in him and he suspected a touch of late autumn Spring Fever. Last year about this time he was trolling the drop-off for Old Ned. But then, that had been a crazy mixed up season anyway. He'd hooked the giant pickerel four times — and lost him each time. In the process, four new lures had disappeared along with an undetermined amount of line. But, a good fight was had by all.

Thoughts of Old Ned brought his spirits up remarkably. Old Ned was the biggest, craftiest, most cantankerous old pickerel Uncle Josh had ever encountered. And the two of them had been encountering each other as far back as Uncle Josh could remember. It had been great sport — but Old Ned had never allowed himself to get caught. This fact did nothing to bolster Uncle Josh's already crestfallen pride.

Now it looked as if Old Ned might live to become a legend after all. Uncle Josh's fishing days had come to a sudden and reluctant halt.

He had been fit to choke with indignation. It was all the fault of that whippersnapper, Dr. McGraw. He'd told Aunt Maude that Uncle Josh would have to confine himself to less active sports, that his heart wouldn't take the excitement Old Ned brought on. It was a conspiracy, Uncle Josh reasoned. They were trying to turn him into a sissy.

As he contemplated some form of rebellion, footsteps approached behind him. He leaned back and closed his eyes.

Aunt Maude's voice always reminded him of a rusty wagon wheel. "Uncle Josh!"

A soft snoring sound was his only reply.

"I'm going to the store for a few minutes—now don't you dare leave the house, hear?"

Uncle Josh waited until he heard the back door slam, then he hurried inside.

A few minutes later he was running down the path toward the dock, his rod and net in one hand, his tackle box in the other.

By the time he had untied the boat and pushed off, his heart was doing the Charleston.

Across the lake, a stiff-legged egret unfolded his wings and lazily took to the air. Uncle Josh cut the motor and drifted close to the great bed of lily pads bordering the drop-off. He unlimbered his casting rod, attached a spoon and shot it far astern.

Shortly afterward he felt the first strike. A small pike. Dangling the fish at arm's length and surveying it through his bifocals, he chirped: "Hi baby! Where's your grandpa today?" Then he released the youngster.

Once again he cast out, propped the rod between his knees and started rowing. He trolled the entire end of the lake. Nothing happened. Just as he was turning the boat, something caught his eye.

Lily pads were acting queerly off his starboard side. Either they parted or were jerked roughly under water. Uncle Josh held his breath. A faint ripple moved on the surface. It became a V-shaped wave, moved into open water and disappeared in a swirl of green foam.

Uncle Josh hardly felt the strike. He reeled in slowly. Suddenly there was a miniature explosion in the water and Uncle Josh's reel reversed itself as the line fairly sizzled back into the water.

"Yahoo!" Uncle Josh was on his feet, waving the doubled rod as if it was a magic wand that had suddenly sprouted wings.

The fish drove toward the lily pads. Uncle Josh leaned back, feeling the violent shivering on the far end of his line. The muscles in his arms cried out in protest and there was a hot, insistent throbbing inside his head as if someone was belaboring him with a frying pan—then suddenly the fish turned, shot out into deep water and sulked.

Uncle Josh wiped his brow with a shaky hand and clamped his teeth together and assumed a scowl of determination.

When the fish moved again it came charging full tilt toward the safety of the lily beds. But Uncle Josh managed to swerve him back into the lake. This time the fish didn't sulk. Instead he just kept going, dragging Uncle Josh and the boat behind him.

The sun beat down unmercifully and the wind had picked up. Uncle Josh was perched in the point of the bow, bracing himself with his knees and wondering what to do next. Halfway across the lake he thought of the anchor. If he could just get that out—

Clamping the curved rod in his left hand he painfully bent down and fumbled with the snarled rope between his feet. Somehow he managed to get it untangled and lifting the cement-filled bucket, he flopped it overboard.

It hit bottom and snagged, the bow dipped dangerously low in the water. The line became rigid with tautness and the wind made it sing. Uncle Josh held his breath and tried to quell the heavy pounding inside him. He felt dizzy and numb all over. Seven polka dots kept dancing in front of his eyes but he flapped his hand and drove them off.

All at once the line went limp and Uncle Josh stood staring at it lying loose on the water. He reeled. It came effortlessly. He peered down into the water and something inside of him got heavy and the polka dots appeared again. Then in the darkness—deep down —a shadow moved. It was heading straight toward the boat and Uncle Josh began cranking the handle of the reel for all his might.

The fish shot under the boat with the speed of an express train.

"Old Ned!" Uncle Josh shouted and executed a kind of ballet step that brought his rod and line around the bow just as the giant pike tightened it and headed for the bottom.

Uncle Josh was staggered by a series of violent bulldog tugs. But finally they grew weaker and weaker and the big fish gave up. Uncle Josh dragged him to the side of the boat and when he saw what he'd caught he almost toppled overboard.

The pike was larger than his wildest dreams. A regular monster. He had difficulty getting it into the boat. But with the fish safely stretched out under the seats, Uncle Josh sagged down and stared at it wide-eyed.

"You confounded ol' cuss, I didn't think I'd ever get you!"

The monster's scared jaws opened and closed weakly.

In between breaths, Uncle Josh cursed and fumed for a while then simmered down and studied his magnificent catch.

"You're finished Ned—you're getting too old for this kind of thing." Gingerly Uncle Josh brought the toe of his shoe near the fish's mouth.

"See there, not even enough teeth to hurt a minnow. Uncle Josh chuckled to himself.

He set back, folded his hands and waited for the old fish to die. Once or twice the large gill covers opened and closed as Old Ned gasped.

Suddenly, Uncle Josh felt very old himself. He glanced down at his hands. He knew Old Ned was watching him. There was a terrible look in those glassy eyes and Uncle Josh reached down and covered them with a clump of seaweed. In a way he felt as if an old friend was passing away. With Old Ned gone—things would not be the same anymore.

Then Uncle Josh made up his mind. He bent down and picked Old Ned up as gently as possible and eased him over the side of the boat into the water.

"I'm going to give you another chance, Ned—I guess neither one of us had a right to be out today. Go on home and nurse your wounds—after all, you're not as young as you used to be and maybe I sort of had the advantage."

Old Ned lay on his side in the water feebly fanning his tail and working his gills. Then slowly he moved off, flipped his tail and made the water boil as he swam away.

Uncle Josh heaved a sigh, removed his glasses and began polishing them. "I won't tell nobody about this," he said. "They might think I'm getting twitty."

Author's comment: *Their war was over when Grandpa felt compassion for the old fish. He always liked to tell us tales about what tough fights he used to have with with him. We all knew how much respect he had for that big pickerel. Grandpa Joe never again fished for Toby.*

7 Military Supplies

Sunflower seeds are excellent for backyard birds, and this seed is the best choice for beginning bird feeding in a variety of feeder styles. Black oil sunflower seeds are the most common and are great for most songbirds, while the larger striped sunflower seeds are suitable for larger birds with stronger bills. Hulled sunflower kernels and chips are also popular with smaller birds because they are easier to eat, though they can be more expensive. Preferred by: Chickadees, house finches, titmice, jays, grosbeaks, cardinals, sparrows, nuthatches, woodpeckers, doves, goldfinches.

Nyjer: Small, thin Nyjer seeds are one of the most popular types of birdseed for small clinging finches. These seeds are exceptionally high in oil, making them great for winter bird feeding. Because of their small size, however, Nyjer seeds can be light and easily spilled or blown away. Mesh-style or sock feeders are best for this expensive seed, and clinging birds will have no trouble feeding from these unique feeders. Preferred by: Goldfinches, purple finches, redpolls, pine siskins, and quail.

Millet: These small white seeds are a common component of birdseed mixes and can be purchased separately for individual feeding if desired. This seed is useful in hopper and tube feeders, as well as for sprinkling on the ground or in tray or platform feeders. Preferred by: Doves, sparrows, juncos, quail, buntings, and wild turkeys.

Safflower Seed: A large, oval seed with a white shell that looks like a plain white sunflower seed, safflower seed has a thick shell and the birds that prefer it need sturdy bills to crack the seeds. **This is a popular seed choice in yards where squirrels often raid feeders, because squirrels do not favor this bitter-tasting seed as readily. It is easy to offer in any feeder type that can accommodate sunflower seeds,** such as hopper, tube, or platform feeders. Preferred by: Cardinals, nuthatches, jays, woodpeckers, house finches.

Cracked Corn: Cracked corn is a less expensive seed often used as filler in birdseed mixes, but its high carbohydrate content makes it suitable for a number of birds, particularly for ground-feeding birds that may have larger appetites. Birds that often feed on grain or are common in agricultural areas may favor cracked corn. This seed can be offered in hopper or tray feeders, or sprinkled directly on the ground for easy access. Preferred by: Sparrows, jays, towhees, grouse, quail, doves, blackbirds, grackles, ducks, and wild turkeys.

Milo: These BB-sized red seeds are not the best choice for most backyard birds, and they are often added to cheap birdseed mixes as a filler. While many birds will simply discard milo seed, it can still be useful for many ground-feeding species with hearty appetites. When these birds visit feeders, offering milo can be a fine way to help save money on birdseed. Because of the seed's medium size, it can be offered in trays, platforms, hoppers, or tube feeders, as well as sprinkled on the ground. Preferred by: Doves, ducks, quail, wild turkeys, and grouse.

How to Choose Quality Birdseed

Not all birdseed is created equally, not even if it is the same type of seed. While birds are not typically picky about the food they eat, higher quality seed will attract more species and will provide better nutrition for healthy flocks. To ensure the seed you buy is a good value and superior quality, look for:

Mix Proportions: If choosing a blend of different seeds, opt for one with a higher proportion of better seeds such as sunflower or millet. Lower quality, less popular mixes often have more fillers like milo and cracked corn, as well as wheat, oats, or other grains birds don't eat as readily.

Freshness: Fresh seed will not have excessive dust, empty hulls, or inedible debris in the mix. Also investigate the seed for any sign of mold, mildew, or insect infestation, such as clumps, webbing, moths, worms, or feces.

Quantity: Larger quantities of birdseed are often a better value at a bulk price. Only purchase seed you can feed to birds before it is stale or spoiled, however, to avoid wasting money on seed that won't be used.

Packaging: Better quality birdseed is often packaged in sturdy plastic or coated paper bags, possibly with easy-to-open tabs or handles for carrying. Look especially for clear packaging that allows inspection of the product before purchase. In some places, you may be able to purchase seed from open bulk containers, allowing close inspection of the seed and letting you get just the quantity you need.

Ingredients: Check the ingredient list on every package of birdseed to ensure it has not been treated with pesticides or insecticides that can be toxic to birds. The list may also name the proportions of seeds used in different blends.

Price: Higher prices do not necessarily mean higher quality seed. Sales are a great way to stock up on a supply of birdseed, and bulk purchases almost always are a better value than smaller packages.

For the last few years I have used a blend of seed that has worked well with my birds. At Amazon, I always order the 40-pound purple colored bag of Vally Splendor Supreme Blend Bird Feed said to contain some nuts, milo and lots of the smaller size black sunflower seeds. We always have the choice of adding to our favorite combinations. For instance, adding a mix of safflower seeds may put the squirrels off their feed since they don't like their taste, but apparently the birds do.

8 All Quiet on the Western Front

One bright mid-August morning at 10:15 AM, carrying a bowl of sliced banana and flakes out to my command post as quietly as possible I opened the back door. Immediately a dozen Red-Winged Blackbirds lifted off the middle lawn in fright, along with a couple Mourning Doves and a dozen more Blackbirds that had been working the feeder's spillover area. I was sorry to have interrupted their late hour breakfasts. One possible drawback to broadcasting handfuls of seed onto part of your lawn is that you may attract four-dozen blackbirds to take up permanent residence in the trees around your lawn. Whenever you go out they all take flight in a huge black cloud until you leave. Then they are back looking for more seed. The only way to discourage this probably is to stop feeding the lawn birdseed for a week or so in the hope that they might go elsewhere looking for food. Usually the squirrels will have gone on to other sources of food and will no longer be starving for birdseed. At least that's my theory. You can always start again when you see the doves out there looking for food.

Anyway, as I came out of the house with my breakfast and upset the Blackbirds, the only one in that scene that had not registered fear was the squirrel I interrupted drinking out of my birdbath. He took his time about leaving. It was Spanky, the youngest and smallest of the Pete brothers. He just looked over his shoulder at me; then calmly stepped to the edge of the bath. Standing on his hind legs looking out at the big green spread of yard he looked like a fellow about to make a world record standing broad jump.

Unruffled, the squirrel sort of half squatted, swung his arms back then forward as he jumped. A beautiful arcing jump in which he landed on all fours and calmly bounced off in the direction of the thickets. I felt sure that he established some kind of record. But it was his calm indifference I liked.

To my right sprawled on the top step of my outdoor white office building lay Spike my tiger-striped Watch-Cat doing what most of his kind did so well that time of day. He yawned; then went back to his catnap. Earlier I had interrupted him halfway to the seed spill area among my bonsai trees in his feline hunting posture, crouched and not moving a hair. He was totally focused on the ground birds picking up seeds. No amount of me telling him, "No," made him move a muscle. He was frozen in full stalk mode. Only when I shuffled my feet did he break form and nonchalantly get up and move off as if it was just what he intended doing and the birds that fled were not even there.

I was seated in my favorite chair at the Command Post earlier at 7:15 A.M., noting daylight brightening and puzzling, as I always did, that there was not a single sound to be heard. Not even a chirp. Where were all the early birds looking for that early worm?

I had just filled the feeder and made enough noise doing it so that any hungry bird, sleeping it off within hearing would know that the time was ripe to feed up.

But not one stirred until I was about through with my coffee when an excited cardinal swooped down and landed on the feeder.

This cardinal may have had a rough night.

Maybe it had just awakened from a great dream. The erect comb flexing and the bird looking this way and that suggested excitement about something. The perky bird quickly polished off a couple sunflower seeds then winged off with much haste. A bird on a mission.

No early bird squirrels were about except for the one enjoying his bath. Most of my backyard wildlife seems to keep banker's hours. Nothing really gets to them before at least 10 in the morning. Then they seem to be everywhere you look, investigating things and snacking.

On the east lawn where I broadcast seeds
a dove and a squirrel search the grass
shoulder to shoulder for feed.

Usually there were a few furry fellows named Pete 1 and
Pete 2 walking around the fall-out seed area looking innocent
as could be. I always watched them closely to see if their eyes
would wander to the base of the pole that led upward to my
bird goodies. But they ignored it as if it were not even there.
Did they know I was watching them?

Three of the Pete brothers chow down on
the overflow seeds, much to my delight.

Surely they did. Did they purposely ignore the prize overhead or were they really thinking, "Why go to all that hassle when the food is right here in front of me?"

The two Petes totally ignored me, which I really appreciated. They ate a few of my offerings and soon moved out onto the lawn to join the now four doves seed-searching in the greens. No one would believe that this time of day was when they really came up with strong attacks, but now my sewing of seeds in the grass and the normal fall-out along the concrete floor of the carport seemed to satisfy their appetites.

As the weeks continued I knew my strategy was working. Between the fall-out and the handouts they were satisfied and willing to co-exist peacefully in our backyard. My sharing had worked. We were at peace! ***Best of all, my birds were not being frightened away from their food. It was intact. It appeared that this arrangement was satisfactory with the squirrels.***

Now, I saw the squirrels in a totally different light. Of course, they had to eat too. The only thing that had made me so mad at them was how they forced their way to the food by cleverly bypassing any of my efforts to stop them. Once I understood the full meaning that they had to eat too, I saw it from their point of view. I provided an extra handful of seed in the grass for them but made them work to get it rather than steal it. I guess the thing that Grandpa learned to have for old Toby…and what I learned to have for my hungry squirrels… came down to just one word – compassion. It said it all… *sympathetic pity and concern for the sufferings or misfortunes of others.* We could all use some of that! Maybe if we did, Man would be less warlike. You would think we'd have figured it out in the time we have been on this planet, but apparently not.

In the weeks and months that followed, I was glad to see

that the squirrels continued to keep the peace. Never again did they make a move to steal food from the feeder. In fact, for one week I never even saw a squirrel. This bothered me until one morning I heard the abrupt sound of something heavy striking the ground under one of our pine trees and I knew exactly what it was.

With the first solid 'Whomp' sound coming from my office pine tree, I knew at once that a squirrel had gnawed free one of the tightly packed, prickly, hard-as-iron young pine cones and failed to balance it on a limb. Squirrels love peeling and eating the tender seeds inside.

Risking being hit on the head with one of these heavy missiles, I looked and found the cone that had just fallen. There was no sign the squirrel had started peeling it yet. I also knew that left to itself, that hand-long thing would still continue to grow opening up and becoming a full grown pine cone just begging to be knocked into some other part of the yard with my riding Deere. To prevent that I pick them all up before mowing. Last Spring this one tree dropped enough to fill two large green garbage bags. All thanks to my squirrels letting them get away. Better they ate them all to their cores. Sure would make a lot less work for me. I don't want any more pine trees either. Oddly, there must have been a shortage of pinecones this year because Our Gang made short work of that big pine's cones.

A couple weeks later I realized that finally, Our Gang was rustling around in the Chinaberry tree getting whatever they eat there. Occasionally, a couple of times, whatever they were getting, got away from them and hit the tin roof of my storage building under it. Whatever it was made a hard noise. This was at the beginning of September.

As we moved more into fall I saw little of the squirrels. I was always there first thing in the morning to fill the feeder and distribute a couple handfuls on the lawn. As usual I wondered why it was so quiet and absolutely nothing, neither man nor beast was stirring at all. Even in No Man's Land.

It's nice having a tranquil scene like this — the view from our Command Post out across the green on the left where the attacks always came from in the past. Now, all is quiet.

As I look across the tops of the Command Post's miniature green trees, out into the large empty green lawn, I sip on my iced coffee and scan the green again, feeling a little alone as I look for any signs of a squirrel…I see nothing but cropped green grass.

Well, maybe tomorrow…. Minutes later out of the corner of my eye I see movement. It's one of the Pete boys cutting across my right lawn coming back from some secret mission.

Next I see him working at the edge of the spillover area, getting breakfast. He knows I am there because he stops and stares at me. Waiting maybe to see if I will bark at him. I wave my hand slowly and say, "Hi." I hope he notices the friendly smile on my face. He goes back to feeding. I do love the sound of peace.

As time passes the peace holds. It is a foggy day in early October when I carry my coffee out the backdoor to my Command Post. The sudden noise as the door opens flushes three doves that were having breakfast at the spillover pile with one of the Pete Brothers.

I instantly regret it. When doves flush their wings make a racket as they literally go from zero to sixty in an instant. The birds swiftly disappear in the fog. The squirrel acts very calm. He stops eating and hops out into the yard, but seems reluctant to leave. I talk softly to him and settle into a chair. He hops toward the thicket and surprisingly goes into his search mode there where I never toss seed.

Feeling sorry for having interrupted his breakfast I broadcast a handful of seed in that area. But he has disappeared into the greenery and nothing moves to show where he has gone. I go back into the house for a small tinfoil pan and place another handful of seed in it and put the pan at the edge of his territory.

Then I sit down behind the forest of little trees and sip my coffee. After a while I peep around my parked car to see if he has found my gift. He hadn't, but the Red-wing Blackbirds found it. Three of them flush as I move the pan under the foliage where they are unlikely to fly. Then I click my tongue to imitate chattering squirrels and softly talk to the invisible squirrel in case he is within hearing. When I get no response I head back to my cup of coffee and fleetingly remember my Grandfather talking to Toby just before he lifted the big fish over the side of the boat and let him go. I had to smile to myself when I thought about me talking to the squirrel like he talked to the fish. Neither Toby nor the squirrel have any idea what we are talking about.

But maybe…just maybe, when Toby realized that he was still alive because Grandpa let him go, and maybe, just maybe, when the squirrel finds the small tinfoil dish of seeds in the thickets where it had not been before, he might understand where it came from.

Hours later, after I finish writing; curious about whether that small handful of birdseed had ever been found by the squirrel, I go and look.

My gift is gone. I pick up the empty foil dish and go back to my command post smiling to myself. This is probably the beginning of more subtle peace offerings. Who knows?

Thank you, Grandpa!

ABOUT THE AUTHOR

Author Robert F. Burgess grew up in Grand Rapids, Michigan. He is an adventure writer/photographer whose books cover a wide range of subjects from underwater archaeology to how to make peace with squirrels. His words make readers feel they are living the adventures he writes about. If you liked this book please give it a rating on **Amazon.com** where you will find many of his other books.

Other Books by Robert F. Burgess Available at Amazon.com

1. To Majorca With Love
2. Real Cliffhangers
3. Hemingway's Paris and Pamplona, Then and Now
4. Meeting Hemingway in Pamplona
5. Florida's Golden Galleons
6. Secret World Of The Sharks
7. Lone Wolf of the Wolfhounds
8. Secrets Of A Happy Hooker
9. Ghost Sniper
10. Return Of The Ghost Sniper
11. Revenge Of The Ghost Sniper
12. The Sweet Goodbye
13. Zapping The Zebra
14. Two For The Marquesas
15. Diving To Adventure
16. Sailing To Adventure
17. Find More Treasure
18. How They Escaped
19. Diving Into The Past
20. They Found Treasure
21. Fire, Ice And Inca Gold
22. Catch More Lobsters
23. Finding Sunken Treasure
24. 1715 Treasure
25. Tracking Treasure By Computer
26. One Night On Scarborough Pond
27. Sniper Up!
28. Charlie, You're Not Perfect
29. Rolling Thunder
30. Carlos Hathcock's Longest Mission

65. Sunken Treasure: Six Who Found Fortunes
66. Handbook Of Trailer Sailing
67. Moving To Majorca
68. Midnights I Remember
69. Best Liked Nam War Stories
70. Tunnel Tales of Our Heroic Tunnel Rats in Vietnam
71. Your Robert F. Burgess Book Sampler
72. Florida Springs From Top to Bottom
73. Tunnel Tales from Vietnam
74. More Tunnel Tales
75. Bermuda Triangle Update
76. The Girl with the Dolphin
77. When Dolphins Came
78. Florida Bahamas Mysteries
79. Flower Power
80. Glass Abstracts
81. Tunnel Secrets of Vietnam
82. Caramelized Stirfry
83. Fountain of Youth
84. Drown Proofing
85. Lone Wolf Snipers and their Tricks
86. Carlos Hathcock: Best Snipers Series
87. Ghost Sniper Collection
88. Hathcock and Burke: Early Nam
89. Diving into the Past
90. Two for the Marquesas
91. What Makes Dolphins Laugh
92. 20,000 Years in a Cave
93. Lost in an Underwater Cave
94. Lindbergh and the Underwater Lake
95. Nam69 Secret Missions
96. Wham! Bam Thank You, Nam
97. Pirate Sniper
98. Animal Pals
99. When Buffalos Fly in Country
100. Sea Cows Have Feelings Too